Exploitation
of Children

Judith Ennew

RSVP
**RAINTREE
STECK-VAUGHN**
PUBLISHERS
The Steck-Vaughn Company

Austin, Texas

Global Issues
Closing the Borders
Crime and Punishment
Exploitation of Children
Genetic Engineering
Gender Issues
Racism
The Rich-Poor Divide
Terrorism
United Nations—Peacekeeper?

Published by Raintree Steck-Vaughn Publishers, an imprint of Steck-Vaughn Company

Library of Congress Cataloging-in-Publication Data
Ennew, Judith.
Exploitation of children / Judith Ennew.
    p.   cm.—(Global issues)
    Includes bibliographical references and index.
    Summary: Discusses issues relating to the exploitation of children including poverty, child labor in agriculture as well as in towns and cities, and hidden forms of child abuse.
    ISBN 0-8172-4546-4
    1. Children's rights—Juvenile literature.
    2. Children—Social conditions—Juvenile literature.
    3. Poor children—Juvenile literature.
    4. Children—Employment—Juvenile literature.
    5. Child abuse—Juvenile literature.
    [1. Children's rights. 2. Poor. 3. Children—Employment.
    4. Child abuse.]
    I. Title. II. Series: Global issues
    HQ789.E56   1996
    305.23—dc20   95-46838

Printed in Italy. Bound in the United States.
1 2 3 4 5 6 7 8 9 0 01 00 99 98 97

Cover: A young boy in Bangladesh breaks up large stones into smaller pieces for building roads.

Title page: A girl working in cornfields in Zimbabwe

Contents page: Nearly two-thirds of Nepal's children work to help their families survive. These two girls are breaking stones to be used as gravel for roads and have no chance to go to school.

Picture acknowledgments

Camera Press 8, 24, 27, 42 (top), 52; Impact 12 (top), 13, 20, 25, 41, 49 (top), 56; Panos *cover* (Zed Nelson), *title page*, 4, 5, 6, 7, 9, 11, 14, 28 (bottom), 29, 30, 31 (both), 32, 33, 34, 37, 38, 39, 44, 46, 47, 50, 53, 55, 57; Popperfoto 16, 17, 18, 58, 59; UNICEF *contents page*, 10, 12 (bottom), 15, 19, 22, 23, 26, 28 (top), 35 (both), 36, 40, 42 (bottom), 45, 48, 49 (bottom), 51

CONTENTS

WHAT IS CHILD EXPLOITATION?

In international law, children are defined as people under 18 years of age. However, what it means to be a child differs both among and within societies. Poor children everywhere have brief childhoods and take on adult responsibilities early. Rich children and most children in wealthier countries spend more time learning to be adults, playing, and going to school. For them the difference between adults and children is very clear. Adults go to work, children go to school. Adults decide what lessons are learned, what clothes are worn, and how to behave. Children depend on adults for food, clothing, and health care as well as education. Adults earn the money to pay for these, and children are not responsible for their own welfare and upkeep. Adults are also expected to protect children from dangers in the streets, bad influences, false information, and exploitation.

Children in rich countries take for granted their comfortable lives. But in poor countries, some children lack even basic necessities such as food and shelter. This homeless boy from Brazil has to depend on charity for a hot meal.

Fact File

The world population of children in 1988

	Adults and children	Under 16 years	Under 5 years
Whole world	5,093,100,000	1,764,300,000	606,200,000
Developing countries	3,897,200,000	1,487,000,000	520,000,000
Developed countries	1,195,900,000	2,773,000,000	86,200,000

These days, most of the world's children live in developing countries, but most of the world's wealth is in developed countries.

Source: *Children and Development in the 1990s: A UNICEF Source Book* (UNICEF)

Fact File

The childhood of Bente Brun, a Norwegian girl

"Bente's breakfast and lunch are prepared for her and her sandwiches placed in her satchel before she goes to school. Some of her classmates, who have the same arrangement at home, complain from time to time when they get sandwiches they do not like: This is no problem in Bente's case. Her mother knows what she likes and she gets the fillings she wants. She also gets what she likes for dinner. Her mother and father are fond of fish, but the children do not like fish, so their mother makes something different for Bente and her brother. The children are used to this special treatment. Bente is also used to being able to wear clean clothes from the closet and to the house being clean and neat without any effort on her part. Her mother does everything in this respect."

Source: Anne Solberg, "Changing Constructions of Age for Norwegian Children" in James, A. and Prout, A., *Constructing and Reconstructing Childhood* (Falmer Press,1990)

Legal differences

The laws that divide adults from children set the ages when children may begin to leave school, start work, drive a vehicle, or have sex. But the main legal difference is when one may vote, which most countries allow at the age of 18. Until then, children are not able to change, or in most cases give their opinions about, the laws and provisions that adults make in what are called the children's "best interests."

The explanation for this difference is that children do not have enough knowledge and experience, so it is believed that they would make bad decisions—and could not understand some kinds of information—and cannot provide for or protect themselves. This was not always the case, and it is still not true of the majority of children in most parts of the world, many of whom are forced to provide for themselves and even for their families.

Most children in wealthier countries enjoy childhood, protected and cherished by their parents, like this girl from Norway, seen with her grandmother.

Developed and developing countries

Although the view of a protected childhood is taken for granted in places like Great Britain and North America, it is actually a relatively recent one and only applies to richer children. These children live mostly in modern, industrial countries called developed countries to distinguish them from poorer, developing countries that are not as industrialized. Wherever they live, poor children are likely to be exploited. This means that some adults, who are richer and thus more powerful, make use of children, force them to work, usually in ways that cause the children harm, and give them little or nothing of the profits. Individual cases of cruel treatment occur when adults exploit children directly; in other cases, children may be exploited in a more general way by a whole industry or by another social group. This can happen in both developed and developing countries.

In developed countries it is often assumed that child labor has been abolished because all children have to go to school. Yet many children are exploited in work outside school hours and during breaks. For example, in England children work in factories, in the United States thousands of children work in agriculture, and in German cities children work as prostitutes.

In developing countries such as Peru, children often work full time. In the countryside there is often no school to go to, and children have to help grow food to eat and sell. In towns and cities, their families need the money they can earn in order to survive. Many boys and girls drop out of school to earn money to see the family through a crisis. Marcos lives in Peru's capital city, Lima. When he was ten years old, his little sister fell seriously ill and there was no money for doctors or medicine. Their father had left home and their mother could not go out to work and leave her daughter

It is not always easy for a child to earn money in an adult world. Like this Brazilian boy, many gain an insecure livelihood by washing windshields for a small amount of money.

(Right) Walking the streets until late at night, carrying a wooden box full of polish and cleaning rags, is hard work. This shoeshine boy from Brazil takes a break from customers who pay him to shine their shoes.

alone. So Marcos decided to earn money himself. Taking a bucket and rag from the house, he set off downtown to wash cars.[1] He was proud to be able to take this responsibility, but he missed school.

Types of exploitation

The case of Marcos shows that children can provide for themselves and take responsibility. But children need education and should be protected from exploitation. Both adults and children can be exploited. At work this can mean that they are not adequately paid. Someone else who controls the situation, such as an employer, takes a bigger share of the money. Marcos had the bucket and rag he needed for work, but he had to find a place where there were cars and a supply of water. He came across an outdoor parking lot for office workers where the caretaker allowed him to use a bathroom faucet. The caretaker exploited Marcos: although he did no work himself, he demanded some of Marcos's money.

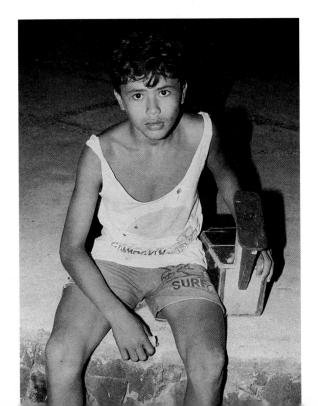

Media Watch

A child's view of exploitation
"People in Lima, Peru, were also asked to take photographs of exploitation. Some adults thought of pictures of slaves or of poor people being badly treated by rich tourists…one child took a photograph of a nail on a wall. 'Few adults understood it, but all the other people were in complete agreement that the picture expressed their feelings in relation to exploitation. The discussion explained why. The simplest work boys engage in at the age of five or six is shining shoes. Obviously, in the barrios [districts] where they live there are no shoes to shine and, for this reason, they must go to downtown Lima in order to find work. Their shine-boxes and other tools of the trade are of course an absolute necessity, and yet these boys cannot be carrying their equipment back and forth every day between work and home. So they must rent a nail on the wall of some place of business, whose owner charges them two or three soles [Peruvian units of money] per night and per nail. Looking at a nail, those children are reminded of oppression and their hatred of it.'"

Augusto Boal in *The Theater of the Oppressed* (Pluto Press,1985)

Exploitation is not just a matter of money. It can occur whenever some people have power over others. Worldwide, but especially in developing countries, large, rich companies have the power to exploit poor, unemployed workers. Rich nations can also exploit poor nations. Some groups in all societies have less power than others; these include women, the poor, and people from certain religious and ethnic groups. Children may be exploited for any of these reasons, but they are also exploited because they are children. In all societies, adults have more power than children. For example, this means that they can pay children less than they would pay adults for the same amount of work and that children cannot complain or demand more money.

The Convention on the Rights of the Child

Since 1989 an international legal instrument, the United Nations Convention on the Rights of the Child, has provided one means of improving the worldwide situation of children.[2] It provides for three kinds of rights for children:

The UN Convention on the Rights of the Child says that children have the right to protection from violence. However, whole families are forced to flee from civil wars and the majority of the world's refugees are children, like these homeless Bosnian boys.

● The right to survival and development, by which governments have the duty to see that all children are provided with welfare, health services, and education, so that they grow into healthy, capable adults.

● The right to protection from abuse, war and conflicts, torture, and harmful forms of punishment, as well as from exploitation.

● The right to participate in decisions made on their behalf, to form associations to represent their own interests, and to express their opinions freely.

Some people feel that exploitation includes all the ways in which children can be harmed and from which they need to be protected. However, this book deals mainly with the

Children have a right to free speech and to organize and promote their own interests. But it is rare to see children taking direct action in defense of their rights, like this demonstration of street children in Rio de Janeiro, Brazil.

Fact File

The United Nations Convention on the Rights of the Child

In 1989 the United Nations (UN) adopted the Convention on the Rights of the Child, which is an international legal document setting out standards that must be achieved by the governments that sign it. The convention took ten years to draft and contains 54 articles setting out the rights to which children should be entitled, including

- a family or family care
- enough food and clean water
- an adequate standard of living
- health care
- special provision for disabled children
- play and leisure
- free education
- safety from abuse
- protection from neglect
- protection from economic exploitation
- protection from war and conflict
- use of the children's own language
- freedom to practice their own religion
- freedom to express their own opinions.

The convention was formally agreed to by more nations, more quickly, than any other United Nations convention. By July 1995, 176 nations had signed and ratified the convention. This means that each country is obligated to impose laws that enforce the 54 articles of the convention and to report regularly to an international committee of 12 experts.

ways children are exploited at work, not only as workers but also as children. Children are particularly vulnerable to being hurt in body or mind, so it can be difficult to be exact about whether a child is being abused or exploited. A girl who works as a maid may not only be exploited by being paid too little and working long hours, but she may also be abused because her employer beats her. She is unlikely to care about the difference. However, the laws relating to exploitation and abuse are different, and children can be protected only if the correct laws are applied. If adults want to help exploited children, or children want to help themselves, they have to be clear about the difference.

THE EFFECTS OF POVERTY

Poverty is difficult to define because everyone knows people richer than themselves and poorer than themselves. In developed countries, poverty is often defined according to the things one cannot afford to buy. It is always possible to think of people with bigger houses, more expensive cars, better clothes, more leisure, and more money to spend on vacations. For children, this also means more toys, better sports equipment, and perhaps a larger collection of videotapes, computer games, or compact discs. But living in a developed country also means that, if parents are unemployed or ill, their children can probably still live in reasonable housing, eat enough food, go to school, and receive treatment if they are ill. Rich countries can afford welfare systems to provide basic services for children, although they do not always do this as well as they might. Thus, most children in developed countries can expect to live to be adults.

Nevertheless, only one in ten of the world's children is lucky enough to live in these countries. In the developing world, 70 of every 1,000 children born will die before their first birthdays. In the poorest countries of all, 114 out of every 1,000 babies will be denied the right to live for even one year. According to the United Nations Children's Fund (UNICEF), 40,000 children a day die before the age of five from illnesses that could easily be prevented or cured, such as diarrhea, measles, and chest infections. The

Fact File

The cost of poverty to children

"Of the thirteen million children dying each year in the world, one-third are African. One out of three children under the age of five dies in Africa. Over 90 percent of all malaria episodes worldwide occur in Africa, claiming over one million lives among the 0–5 aged population each year. Childhood blindness affects about 1.5 million children worldwide. Of these, the majority of cases occur in Africa."

Source: Dr. Remi Sogunro, *The Health Advisor, Santé Salud* (Plan International, 1993)

Sudden disasters leave poor parents even less able to care for their children. In 1994 huge numbers of families fleeing terrible violence in Rwanda arrived in the neighboring country of Zaire, but they found little food or shelter in hastily built refugee camps.

When parents cannot afford a proper house, children have to live in makeshift shantytowns like this one in Brazil.

underlying causes are lack of food, dirty water, poor sanitation, and insufficient health care.[3]

Poverty also means being less able to protect your family from economic and political changes, conflict, and disaster. The poor do not have anywhere to go when disaster strikes. They cannot afford to rebuild their houses if they are destroyed.

Poverty makes people vulnerable to exploitation because it makes them powerless. They cannot afford to bargain for better wages or conditions. They need a job today because they must have the money for the next meal.

Migration to cities

The main causes of poverty in developing countries are rapid population growth and damage to the environment. When too many people rely on farming the same land, they soon use up the area's natural resources. Crops fail and people cannot find enough fuel. Many families are forced to travel to towns and cities to find work.

Wealth and poverty are starkly contrasted in large cities. Here, people live in poverty in a slum on the outskirts of Bombay, India, within sight of high-rise buildings in the city.

Bangkok, the capital of Thailand, is rapidly growing into a modern high-rise city. As far as 14-year-old Sairoong is concerned, this does not mean enjoying modern conveniences. She spends her life breathing the dust of building construction. She has not been able to go to school because her parents regularly move from one construction site to another to find work.

In a shantytown on the outskirts of Lima, Peru, a child turns cartwheels amid the dust and garbage. There is no space for him to play in the straw hut where he lives.

All over India, children, like these boys in Mysore, can be seen living and working on construction sites for roads and buildings.

Media Watch

Children of construction workers in Thailand

"Seventy-three percent of children belonging to families of construction site workers [in Thailand] are malnourished. Very few have received schooling and most are in danger of abuse because of frequent quarrels within the family.

"Working on a construction site is hard. Families live in small corrugated huts next to the site. Younger children are left at home from early morning, when both mother and father go to work.

"The location changes also. When the job is finished, the workers dismantle their huts and move to the next site. Children suffer from this transient existence. They follow their parents here and there, not knowing their future. The hopes and dreams of children belonging to construction site workers are simple: they wish for a stable life and a happy family."

Child Workers in Asia,
Volume 3, No. 2, 1987

Sairoong can still remember the rural village where she was born, with its green fields and fresh air, as well as the many relatives who lived there. Shortage of water to irrigate the fields caused the rice crop to dry up, and they did not even have enough to feed themselves, let alone to sell. The family was forced to make the long journey south to Bangkok. At first it was difficult for Sairoong to get used to playing among the piles of cement blocks on the construction sites. Now that she is older, she works carrying cement, wood, and heavy metal reinforcements from 7:30 A.M. until late afternoon. She also has to prepare the meals for the whole family.[4]

Towns and cities are home to rich and poor people. Shantytowns ring the modern centers of Indian cities where makeshift homes stand in every available space, including the sidewalks. Families live without water, sanitation, and electricity in shacks made of cardboard and plastic sheeting right next to modern apartment buildings and offices.

This family lives on a garbage dump in the Philippines, scraping a meager living from other people's trash.

Sona has lived all her 12 years in a slum in New Delhi, India. Her life shows the effects of poverty on children: working, being always hungry, living in insecure housing, and not going to school. She wakes before daybreak to clean the family hut, light the fire, cook, and feed the family before she leaves to work on a garbage dump, looking for pieces of iron or plastic that she can sell. Her father spends most of the little money she earns on alcohol. Sona is permanently hungry and always feels sick. This is not surprising. Her home has neither water nor sanitation. She is exposed to infections every day as she picks over rotting garbage, often getting cut by hidden objects. It is a wonder that she has not yet become seriously ill. Of course she does not go to school.[5]

Sona gives her brothers more food than she eats herself. Boys are always favored over girls

Media Watch

Infant mortality on rise in wealthy United States
"More babies die in infancy in America than any other industrialized country, despite an expenditure of 11.5 percent of U.S. earnings on health care, says *The Health of America's Children,* published by the Children's Defense Fund, a welfare organization based in Washington, D.C.

"The report, which received scant attention in the U.S. press, places America nineteenth in the world, behind countries including Singapore and Spain. For blacks, the U.S. [infant] mortality rate was worse than Cuba, Costa Rica, or Bulgaria. In Washington, Boston, Chicago, or Philadelphia, a black baby is more likely to die before its first birthday than a baby born in Jamaica…

"A main reason for America's poor record is the high cost of medicine. More than 35 million Americans have neither health insurance nor the money for treatment they need. This aggravates the high infant death rate because millions of women do not see their doctors. They cannot afford to pay fees that can exceed $50 for one visit."

Christopher Reed in the *Guardian*, November 1988

Adults and children compete on this garbage dump in São Paulo, Brazil, seeking scraps of food or any useful items to sell.

in India, and many girls suffer from malnutrition as a result. This does not always mean outright starvation and death but the constant problem of never having enough to eat or having the right kinds of food. The effects of malnutrition on children are permanent exhaustion, the inability to think quickly, losing the will to make an effort to improve their lives, and ultimately growing into smaller, weaker adults. Girls are particularly likely to suffer the effects of poverty, but so are boys and girls from certain groups. For example, Indian society is divided into castes, according to the work people do. If you are born into a low caste, like Sona, you will almost certainly be poor all your life. Even in developed countries, skin color or being part of a less powerful group can bring disadvantages for children. Children of migrant families, gypsies, and nonwhite parents tend to have poorer health care, worse education, and less of a chance to grow up to have good jobs and powerful positions in society. They are also more likely to be exploited, sometimes even by their own parents.

Children making bricks in Islamabad, Pakistan, are forced to work as bonded laborers to pay off family debts to the factory owner.

Paying off debts

Parents often find it impossible to make ends meet, even if children are working with them. Then they are forced to take out loans, usually to see the family through a crisis, such as food shortage or medical care, but also to pay for family events such as weddings or funerals. Moneylenders charge high rates of interest and also accept repayment in labor. Thus, children are often sent to work for the moneylender until the debt is paid off.

This system is called bonded labor and is recognized by the United Nations as a form of slavery. It is illegal everywhere, but is widespread throughout south Asia. In India it is one of the leading causes of child labor. Almost 73 percent of child laborers are put to work by their own parents or guardians. In some villages landlords depend entirely on the bonded labor of children to carry out the farmwork. Loans may have to be taken out afresh as new crises hit families, so the debts may rise rather than being paid off. Some children find themselves starting a lifetime of slavery, with debts they may pass on to their own sons and daughters.

Bonded labor illustrates how easy it is to exploit the poor. When parents have neither land nor money, their children become their only wealth, the only thing they have to trade for survival. But bonded labor also shows the unique powerlessness of children, who can be bought and sold in this way by their own parents.[6]

Selling children

Some parents even sell their children directly. Babies are sold for adoption by desperately poor parents, particularly young single mothers. Childless couples from rich countries are able to pay to adopt children from poor families. There are two levels of exploitation involved, because there is usually a go-between or broker who makes the arrangements between the rich couple and the poor parents. Although not all international adoptions are conducted in a way that exploits people, some brokers make large profits.[7]

British couple Bernadette and Adrian Mooney with their adopted daughter, Grace, a Romanian orphan. In July 1994, the Mooneys were convicted of trying to smuggle another baby girl out of Romania, having bought her from her Romanian parents.

Media Watch

Romanians jail baby smugglers

"Lawyers acting for a Berkshire [England] couple sentenced to two years and four months in prison by a Bucharest court yesterday for trying to smuggle a baby to Great Britain are to seek a pardon from the Romanian president…

"…Mr. and Mrs. Mooney, ages 41 and 39, adopted their Romanian-born daughter, Grace, in 1991. They were arrested at the Hungarian border on July 2 [1994] with a five-month-old Romanian gypsy baby, Monica, sedated and hidden in a box in their car.

"Three men convicted of arranging the sale of the baby were imprisoned for two years and eight months, and the baby's unmarried 17-year-old parents will serve a year's sentence once they turn 18."

The *Guardian*, October 1994

In other cases, older children are sold. Once again, a broker is usually involved. The parents are mostly from rural areas and do not know what will happen when their son or daughter goes to the city with the broker. They probably desperately need money to pay off debts, and the broker will tell them that the child will be able to work and make lots of money to help the whole family. In reality the work is likely to be in an illegal sweatshop where the children sleep, eat, and work, toiling many hours for little or no wages; or, worse still, working as prostitutes in a brothel. Children from rural northeast Thailand travel to the southern capital, Bangkok, while up to 7,000 children are reported to be sold over the border between Nepal and India every year to work in carpet factories and brothels.[8]

Very few of the estimated seven million child bonded laborers in south Asia are ever freed from their slavery. The effects of their suffering show on the faces of these Indian children, who were freed by the Bonded Labor Liberation Front.

Media Watch

The promise to children

"On Sunday, September 30, 1990, a great promise was made to the children of the 1990s. On that day, 71 presidents and prime ministers came together for the first World Summit for Children. It was the largest gathering of heads of state and government in history. And the outcome was an extraordinary new commitment—a decision to try to end child deaths and child malnutrition on today's scale by the year 2000, and to provide basic protection for the normal physical and mental development of all the world's children.

"This overall goal was broken down into more than 20 specific targets listed in the Plan of Action agreed on by the 159 nations represented at the summit. All governments will review their plans and budgets and decide on national plans of action before the end of 1991.

"'We are prepared to make available the resources to meet these commitments,' said the final Declaration. All national and international organizations have been asked to participate. In particular, the worlds of religion, education, communications media, business, and nongovernmental organizations in every country are invited to join this decade-long effort."

UNICEF, *The State of the World's Children,* 1991

CHILD WORK AND CHILD LABOR

Throughout history, children have worked alongside their parents, gathering wild fruits, digging the fields, tending animals, and helping in stores and craft workshops. With the development of industry, children began to work outside the home without the protection of their families becoming child laborers in mines and factories. It took many years of protest and reform for the worst of this kind of exploitation to be abolished and universal compulsory schooling to be established. Yet, even now, most children work. In developed countries they go to school and learn the skills that will later benefit both themselves and the rest of society; they run errands, help to cook, clean the house, and do part-time jobs such as newspaper delivery. Many also help out in family businesses, workshops, and farms. Often they work by choice to make extra pocket money for things they want or to help put themselves through college. In developing countries, most children work because they have to in order to survive.

Well before dawn, this Rwandan girl begins collecting firewood so that her family can cook. This is a daily task for rural children in developing countries. The children sometimes walk many miles before breakfast.

Fact File

Child work or child labor?

According to the International Labor Office, the difference between child work and child labor is that child laborers are:

- Working too young—children in developing countries often start work at the age of six or seven.

- Working long hours—in some cases 12 to 16 hours a day.

- Working under strain—physical, social, or psychological—in mines, for example, or sweatshops.

- Working on the streets—in unhealthy and dangerous conditions.

- For very little pay—as little as $3 for a 60-hour week.

- With little stimulation—dull repetitive tasks, which stunt the child's social and psychological development.

- Taking too much responsibility—which inhibits self-confidence and self-esteem, as with slave labor and sexual exploitation.

Source: *World Labor Report 1992* (International Labor Office, 1992)

Child work is not bad in itself. Children are less likely to be exploited if they work with their families and learn skills they can use in adult life. It is work outside the family that puts children in greatest danger of exploitation.

Children are often employed because they can be paid less than adults for doing the same job. Newspaper delivery, for example, is usually regarded as working for pocket money; few adults would agree to be paid so little. Children who work part time in supermarkets or fast-food restaurants are also usually paid very low wages. Yet, as one 16-year-old English girl says, "We are people too, and should not be treated like slaves just because we are children."[9]

The dangers of work

A further problem is that these jobs may bring hidden dangers, especially for the young. English law states that children under sixteen years old should not work before 7:00 A.M. or after 7:00 P.M., but most newspaper deliveries start at around 6:00 A.M. and children bicycling around in the dark are often involved in accidents.[10]

Thirteen-year-olds in the United States are allowed to start part-time work. Often their first jobs are as newspaper delivery people.

66 99

• • •

Fifteen-year-old Pedro is an illegal immigrant from Mexico living in the United States. He has a job washing dishes in the Soup Bowl Cafe, where he was never asked for his work permit or social security number. He is paid $2.85 an hour and works three nights a week and Sunday mornings.

"It's supposed to be $3.10 [the minimum wage in 1979], but my boss can't pay me that much right now because he doesn't have a big company and he can't afford it. I take home a little over a hundred dollars every fifteen days."

Sheila Cole, *Working Kids on Working* (Lothrop, Lee and Shepard Books, 1980)

In the United States, it is both legal and common for children over 14 years of age to stock shelves and work at the checkouts of groceries. In large supermarkets, goods are stacked high to save space and shop workers risk falling off ladders or being crushed by a falling pile of boxes. Children are also injured opening boxes with sharp knives. Although the law says that children cannot operate the machines that are used to crush and bale these boxes, an 11-year-old boy from New York City was killed in December 1988 when he became entangled in a box-crusher.[11]

Child labor laws are similar everywhere, yet seldom strictly applied. In developing countries, where the need for an income is greater, the danger of exploitation is higher. A few children are obliged to work because they live on their own. Others have parents who may be unemployed, can find only occasional work, or have jobs that do not pay enough to provide for the whole family.

Media Watch

"In Norfolk [England], where it is estimated that about 5,000 children work in fields and on farms, dozens are employed illegally. In 1991 children as young as ten were found cutting the tops off carrots for 30p (about 50¢) a crate. The crates held 600 carrots, and smaller children had to stand on boxes to reach the worktops.

"When an 18-year-old went into the hospital for an operation on a protruding disc in his back he was told the injury was due to the three years he had spent as a paperboy. Just unlucky, or seriously underprotected? Newspapers for a Sunday round can weigh anything up to 70 pounds, but post office workers are not allowed to carry bags weighing more than 28 pounds."

Ruth Fisher, "Growing up," from the *Observer*, May 1994

Fact File

Which countries have the most child workers?
No one is sure how many children work, because child laborers are largely hidden from the world. This is what the International Labor Office said in 1993:

● Asia has the highest numbers of child workers—44 million in India alone.

● Latin American countries have up to 26 percent of children at work.

● African countries have up to 20 percent of children at work.

● In Europe, high concentrations of children work in Italy, Spain, and the United Kingdom.

● In the United States hundreds of thousands of children work in agriculture, fast-food restaurants, and garment factories.

Source: *World Labor Report* (International Labor Office, 1993)

Combining work and school

Marcos (see page 7) had to go out to work when his sister was ill—Peru is too poor to provide financial support for unemployed adults and there is virtually no free health care. Marcos had to leave school, but some children are able to combine work and education. There are so many children in developing countries that schools often operate morning, afternoon, and sometimes evening shifts. It is possible for a child to go to work in the morning and to school in the afternoon. This means very long days—getting out of bed for work while it is still dark and returning home at lunchtime to change for school. In the evenings there is homework to do and probably household chores such as collecting water, cooking, washing, and cleaning. Many working children do not go to bed until very late and then have only four or five hours of sleep before the whole long day begins again.

Working children often cannot find the time to go to school, so schools go to them. Child ragpickers in New Delhi, India, take advantage of space in a local shrine to have classes with teachers from an educational organization called Butterflies.

In the shifting world of construction workers, children's education is often disrupted. Informal schools on construction sites, like this one in India, may be the only chance for the children to learn to read and write.

The law in almost every country says that children must go to school and that education is free. However, there is not enough money for schools, especially beyond the elementary level, to be built everywhere. Children from the countryside move to towns in order to continue their educations. Their families cannot send money for their upkeep, so they work their way slowly through school—if they are lucky. It costs money to register at the beginning of the year, and uniforms are expensive, as are books, notebooks, pens, and other equipment. In addition, every moment spent in school is time that could have been spent earning money. Some families never manage to save the money to register their children for school.

The effects of war

When societies are in turmoil, because of war or internal fighting, schools may not be able to open, or the buildings may have to be used to shelter families who have lost or fled their homes. This kind of disturbance particularly affects children. Sometimes their parents are unable to look after them, and sometimes they are separated from their families in the confusion. Children become particularly vulnerable to exploitation, not only as victims of violence but also by becoming involved in the fighting as soldiers. This is one way for children who can no longer rely on their parents to obtain food, money, shelter, and adult protection. In 1994 children were either soldiers or actively involved in fighting in 27 countries around the world.[12] One was 12-year-old Abdoul Raouf, a soldier in the civil war in Afghanistan, who found his machine gun too heavy to carry for more than three minutes at a time. His duty was to guard a control post, inspecting cars and confiscating arms, money, food, and drugs. He had already killed three men.[13]

Children are not only exploited in factories and on the streets. They are often forced to fight in adult wars and conflicts they do not understand. This boy in Chad, central Africa, is too young to vote but he is a government soldier fighting in the civil war.

Some child soldiers do not consider that they are exploited; they claim that they are freedom fighters and have a right to defend their own people. The only part of the UN Convention on the Rights of the Child that treats people under 18 years old as adults is Article 18, which says that children over 15 years of age may take a direct part in fighting. This is contradictory if you consider that all other kinds of dangerous work are forbidden to people of the same age.

Children are soldiers in both developed and developing countries. Three 17-year-old British boys died in the brief war between Great Britain and Argentina in 1982; they were not entitled to vote, but they were allowed to fight.[14]

Little is known about the long-term effects of the brutality of war on children, such as the effect on Abdoul of killing three people before he was 12 years old. Children are developing in mind and body. What happens in childhood will affect their whole lives. It is known that children suffer more from exploitative work than adults do. Because children are paid less, they often have to work longer to earn the same money. Working with tools and machines designed for adults is tiring and dangerous and can damage their growth. Children's smaller bodies absorb greater concentrations of poisonous fumes and chemicals, which can cause fatal diseases such as cancer. Their sight and hearing are more easily affected by working in poor light or in continuous loud noise. This damage can be lifelong.

Protecting child workers
Parents do not always know that some working conditions are harmful and may not be able to protect their children. The International Labor Organization has tried to clarify the difference between child work and child labor by saying

This boy is a soldier in the Karen National Liberation Army, fighting a civil war against the government of Myanmar (formerly Burma) in 1988.

that children should not work for too long or too hard, but no one has yet done any research to find out what "too hard" or "too long" really mean for children of different ages.

Some people think that all children should be banned from doing any work. Two recent campaigns involved importing carpets and clothing made with cheap child labor into developed countries. These products compete with more expensive products made by adults. One proposed law in the United States, called the Harkin Bill after Senator Tom Harkin (D-Iowa) who introduced it in 1993, said that adult workers in the United States "should not have their jobs imperiled by imports produced by child labor in developing countries."[15] Harkin aimed to ban imports of carpets and cloth made by children under 15 years of age. Some European countries have considered similar laws. Organizations such as Anti-Slavery International campaign against carpets made by children; their primary aim is to combat exploitation of children rather than to protect adult jobs.

Carpet and clothing exports to Europe and North America represent up to half the foreign earnings of countries such as Bangladesh and India. Even though the Harkin Bill was not passed, some factories responded to the fear of

Media Watch

"Developed countries led by the United States and France have sought to link international trade to social issues such as 'internationally recognized labor standards and practices.' At the Marrakesh GATT ministerial conference in April 1994, these countries wanted the social issue to form a part of the future work program of the World Trade Organization.

"Many in the developing countries ask why is it that it is only now that the conditions of child labor are pricking the consciences of the United States and other developed countries.

"Is it because of the joblessness of the 1990s, that governments in industrialized countries fear the effects of cheap imports on employment? ...

"Why is the concern about child labor only in the industrial export sector? Why is there no concern for the agriculture, service, and informal sectors, where child labor is more prevalent? And who, by the way, is to define what is and what is not child labor?"

Ranjan Poudyal, *International Efforts to Ban Products That Use Child Labor in South Asia: SARO Briefing Paper No. 1* (Save the Children,1994)

Children begin work weaving carpets as young as three years old. Afghanistan is famous for the carpets it exports all over the world, often made by children. These Afghan children still work on weaving, even though they are in exile in Pakistan.

(Left) Carpet weaving means concentrating on the pattern and sitting in an uncomfortable position for hours. A boy studies a carpet design as he weaves on a loom in Kathmandu, Nepal. He earns only about 40¢ a day, even though the carpet industry is a major source of income for Nepal.

losing these profitable markets by firing their child workers. Unfortunately, children who lose their jobs do not necessarily cease to work. They need an income, so they simply find other ways of earning a living, which could be even more exploitative, such as prostitution.

A group of carpet manufacturers in India responded to these campaigns by setting up a labeling system called RUGMARK, which proves that child labor is not used to make their goods. The manufacturers are obliged to pay a license fee, which is supposed to be used to help child laborers. However, there is no inspection system and no formal plans about how to use the money.[16]

Although such projects and campaigns exist, they do not seem to have much effect on the lives of working children. The concerns of the Harkin Bill and the RUGMARK plan are those of adults. No one asks the opinions of working children, most of whom do not make carpets but labor in agriculture, in domestic service, and in selling goods and services on the city streets of developing countries. Despite these campaigns, there are no worldwide systems to help child laborers.

WORKING IN AGRICULTURE

In the twentieth century, more people live in towns and cities than ever before. The increase has been vast. In developed countries, up to 80 percent of the people now live in urban areas, using the countryside for leisure if they visit it at all. Most of what people know of rural life comes from movies and television shows; these tend to give a romantic picture of leafy countryside and traditional homes.

Rural life

More children work in agriculture than in any other type of work, but this is often seen as acceptable because it is believed that they work alongside relatives and learn skills for adult life. Traditional rural work has a romantic image, especially when viewed from the town. People tend to think of work like goatherding, sheepherding, sowing seeds, and harvesting as being less difficult and more healthy than, for example, factory work. Although this kind of rural labor may give its

Goatherding in Mexico may seem to be a healthy and quaint country life for a child, but, besides missing school, this boy will spend hours away from home, with nobody to talk to.

A boy helps his father tend their small farm in the Chiapas region of Mexico. Children all over the world help their parents grow enough food for the family to survive.

(Left) Two girls harvesting coffee beans in Guatemala. Agricultural workers often have to travel to obtain seasonal work. For example, every year thousands of adults and children travel from Guatemala into Mexico to work on the coffee harvest.

workers more fresh air and variety of tasks than city work, it is still hard, demanding labor.

Farm work becomes harder if droughts, floods, or landslides destroy crops and animals. Unskilled work tends to be performed by children. As life in the country becomes more difficult, children work harder, traveling farther in search of water or firewood or taking animals far away in search of grass. Their chances of having time for school become slimmer, even if there is a school close to home.

The image of family farms does not match the reality of modern rural life in both developed and developing countries. Increasingly, farming is being taken over by big farms that are run as businesses. Rural children still work alongside their parents, but not on their own farms. The whole family group is exploited by the owners of huge areas of farmland and large plantations.

This is true in developed and developing countries. There are four million migrant and seasonal agricultural workers in the United States. Wherever farming requires many workers, mostly Latin American and black families, including over one million children, are found. These children account for a disproportionate share of deaths and disabling injuries in agriculture.

The dangers of farmwork

Farmwork is dangerous and largely unregulated. Child labor laws for agriculture are particularly loose and badly applied. In the United States even children under 12 years old can legally work on farms under certain circumstances. They work because their parents are paid low wages or in piecework—by the quantity of fruit or vegetables harvested or by rows of crops thinned or weeded. The work of every family member is needed to meet the day's target and earn enough money to live.[17]

At harvest time in the vineyards of California, children of migrant families join their parents in the seasonal task of picking grapes.

Media Watch

"Jeris and Otto Petersen, who have a 500-acre farm in Corning, Iowa, were always extremely cautious around farm equipment, especially where their six sons were concerned. Their oldest two, Justin and Shaun, were both very responsible and eager, but the Petersens always made sure the boys could thoroughly handle a task before letting them attempt it alone. Even so, harsh economic reality dictated that the boys do their share: to keep the family farm, the family had to work together…

"On July 10, 1989, [Shaun] was helping his dad run a sweep auger, which pulls corn from the floor of the cement silo. 'The auger looks like a big screw,' explains Jeris. 'As it moves in a circle, it pulls in the corn.' Shaun volunteered to go inside the silo and shovel the corn in front of the auger to speed up the process. Although he almost always wore knee boots, that day he was wearing high-top sneakers. One of his shoelaces got caught in the sweep of the auger, and he was pulled into the spinning blades. His whole body was shattered."

Rosalind Wright in *Family Circle,* December 1991

Children are particularly useful in unskilled farm work, such as weeding and harvesting, but they can be harmed by using tools that are too big for them or by lifting heavy produce. The most common cause of injuries is the use of tractors and other farm machinery, not just from the machines themselves but also from the noise, dust, and chemicals used. A 1992 survey showed that nearly a third of farm boys in the United States are driving tractors by the time they are about eight years old. If children become tired by working long hours, the risks of accidents with machinery are greater. In 1988 a 14-year-old boy was still cutting hop vines at 2:30 A.M. Exhausted, he lay down to sleep and did not see the truck that ran him over and crushed him to death.[18] Even without such tragedies, fatigue due to long working hours affects school performance and thus has bad effects in adult life.

This boy is burning a field of stubble after the sugarcane harvest on a plantation in Honduras. If the fire were to get out of control, he would be in great danger.

Child agricultural workers often use machines and tools that are dangerous. This boy is using a large, sharp knife to cut sugarcane in Guatemala.

Fact File

Child agricultural workers in the United States
"The Washington Association of Apple Growers [1989] surveyed 614 farmers in central Washington—568 orchard owners and the rest vegetable and hop growers. More than 98 percent of these growers reported employing minors [under 18 years old]—more than 2,500 children in all, and 73 percent used children under 16 years of age. Almost 97 percent of these children were working with older family members.

"The number of hours worked per week during the school year ranged from 4 to 32, with 86 percent reporting less than 24 hours per week. During the summer months, children worked 20 to 55 hours per week. Almost 80 percent of the respondents said the minors worked a 40-hour week."

Source: Valerie A. Wilk, "Health Hazards to Children in Agriculture" in *The American Journal of Industrial Medicine*, 1990

Perhaps the most dangerous part of modern farming for children is the use of chemicals to kill weeds and insects. Children of migrant farmworkers throughout the United States not only work unprotected in fields that are still damp with dangerous chemical spray or even while the crops are sprayed from tractors or airplanes, but they also live in camps that are sprayed with pesticides. Their families are so poor that they move from camp to camp according to the growing season of various crops, living in crowded and unsanitary housing. It is difficult to obtain medical care, and their schooling is repeatedly interrupted.[19]

(Left) This boy is spraying insecticides onto potatoes in Java, Indonesia. He has no protection from the dangerous chemicals he is using.

On rubber plantations in Malaysia, latex—the liquid collected from rubber trees—is put into a mixture of acid and water to solidify. This boy's work involves removing the rubber from the mixture with his bare hands.

Johnny Ramirez worked picking grapes in California. This hurt his back because he had to carry crates weighing 20 pounds down the long fields, although he only weighed 75 pounds himself. But the worst part was that his sweat washed the sulfur used to dust the grapes into his eyes, making them burn.[20]

Large estates and plantations, where only one crop is grown and whole families live and work for low wages, are particularly dangerous places for children. The owners make heavy use of chemicals because they cannot afford to lose a whole year's crop to insects and plant diseases. Besides living in an area contaminated with these poisons, children may be employed to spray the chemicals without protective clothing.

The Malaysian economy depends on exporting rubber and palm oil from huge plantations. Thirteen-year-old Murugan and his 12-year-old sister, Padma, work spraying pesticides onto seedling rubber plants. "Our father said he didn't have enough money to send us to the secondary school in town and wanted us instead to work on the plantation. Sometimes my sister and I cry when we see other children from the plantation going to school. I guess we'll spend all our lives here among the rubber trees," says Murugan. It is also likely that contact with the chemicals will shorten their lives.[21]

An invisible problem

The use of child workers to keep labor costs low is repeated all over the world wherever agricultural production requires large numbers of unskilled workers. In Tanzania the government owns many estates growing sisal, a plant that is used to make rope. Children work on these estates from the age of ten, but only in the activities that require many unskilled laborers. They transplant and weed small plants, carry wet sisal fibers from the machines to the drying lines, and collect the short fibers that are thrown out of the brushing machines. They are paid half the adult wage. As children form nearly a third of the labor force this means that the industry is able to save 15 percent on the wage bill. These children work 11 hours a day, six days a week, with no proper rest periods. Many suffer from lung diseases because the manufacturing process produces a lot of dust. But the worst problem is the way the children's skin itches from the liquid that oozes from the plants and into the cuts on their hands, caused by the needle-sharp points of sisal leaves.[22]

The work of children in agriculture is important for all countries, but their contribution is seldom acknowledged and relatively little is known about this exploitation. It is as if child farmworkers were invisible—it is assumed that they are working with their families and will come to no harm. Campaigns against child labor tend to concentrate on child work in factories or on the streets, so that most information is about child labor in towns and cities, even though far more children toil on the land.

Child workers in agriculture are often ignored by campaign organizations. In Senegal, the vast majority of child workers are in rural areas, like these Mauritian refugees transplanting rice seedlings. Much more attention is paid to the problem of child workers in towns.

CHILD WORK IN TOWNS AND CITIES

For rural migrants, cities offer the hope of a better life, jobs, schools, health care, and entertainment. The reality is pollution, traffic fumes, and piles of uncollected garbage. Migrants often have to live in slums and shantytowns, where water is bought from trucks that arrive only irregularly and sewage runs in the streets. If they cannot find a place to live they will be forced to build makeshift shacks from whatever is available to them. Children are particularly vulnerable to illness and accidents in these living conditions. There may be no school nearby, or none they can afford to attend. Parents often cannot find jobs

(Above) Selling on streets can be lonely and boring. This girl is selling soft drinks in Thailand.

(Right) The reality of life in towns and cities can be as bleak as this wooden town on stilts in the city of Iquitos, Peru.

or are paid very low wages. Thus, poor children in urban areas usually have to work.

Like their parents, deprived city children are most likely to have jobs in what is called the informal sector, which is insecure and not regulated by employment laws. Working on the street is the most visible informal sector work. Children may provide a service like Marcos does (page 7), taking his bucket and rag to wash cars, or they may sell goods. Children work in a variety of ways in cities throughout the developed and developing worlds.

Fact File

"The rise in urban populations is linked to an increase in the pollution of air, water, and land. Air is polluted by factories as well as by fires used to heat homes and cook. Water is polluted by household sewage, garbage, factory waste, and debris from construction sites. Land is polluted by garbage and industrial waste, which may simply be dumped in enormous landfills, where rats and other vermin gather.

"Because towns and cities are now so large, people have to travel long distances to work. Transportation causes some of the worst pollution. Up to 40 percent of an urban area may actually be taken up by road networks. Buses, cars, and trains produce huge quantities of waste metals, plastics, and rubber. But the worst problem of all is air pollution from exhaust pipes."

Source: Cristina Szanton Blanc, *Urban Children in Distress* (Gordon and Breach, 1994)

It may look haphazard, but ragpicking is big business. This Brazilian boy knows exactly what he is looking for, whom he can sell it to, and how much he needs to collect in order to survive.

In Dhaka, the capital of Bangladesh, a street boy recycles the city's garbage and scrapes a bare living for himself.

Ragpicking

Another common trade for city children is ragpicking—searching in other people's trash for things they can sell. Ragpicking is big business even though it is dirty and often dangerous. Not all children collect garbage from dumps like Sona (page 14). In other parts of India, children roam the streets in groups, collecting large bags of trash, which they spread out on the sidewalk to sort and then take to sell in recycling centers.

Ragpickers are essential to the recycling process, which is important both for the urban economy and for keeping towns relatively clean. For children, ragpicking often results in chest and eye infections as well as cuts and skin allergies. It is also hard work. In order to survive, ragpickers in Bombay, India, have to make at least 20 rupees [65¢] a day, which means collecting a stack of paper about three feet high. They also have to pay adults who exploit them, such as powerful slumlords who take a cut of their earnings, or police who arrest children on false charges and then demand money for their release.[23]

Media Watch

Victims of fireworks narrate their woes

"Shankareswari, age ten, used to work in a fireworks factory in Tamil Nadu [formerly Madras], India. Leaving her home at 6:00 A.M. in the company bus, working more than 12 hours in the most noxious ambience [poisonous environment], handling dangerous explosives, this girl child would return home late at night just to supplement the family income by thirty rupees [about a dollar] a week. The children only get a break to take lunch, which they carry with them.

"She said most of the children, including herself, complain of stomach and eye problems. She witnessed a blast in the factory in which many died or were crippled."

Hindustani Times, November 1994

Employment in workshops

Not all urban children work on the streets. Others find employment in small workshops, where goods are made or mended. Jobs in car and bicycle maintenance are much sought after by boys, many of whom work after school for no pay in order to learn skills for adult life. But some children work all day, do not go to school, and may even sleep on the workshop floor. Machinery is old and unsafe, and the workshops themselves are small with poor light and air full of dust and poisonous fumes. Whole industries in the Far East depend on cheap child labor in small workshops, particularly for making clothing and toys for export to developed countries. Children are employed because they can be paid less than half the adult wage.

Workshop owners are often under contract to large companies. This means their own profits are small, so they prefer to use cheap child labor. This is the case in the Thai leather bag industry, which has won prizes for exports. The factories are organized in small units, each under the control of an adult. Thirteen-year-old Suriyan had not planned to work making bags, but a subcontractor came to his village and

Working in a blacksmith's shop in Vietnam, this boy is exposed to dust and injury, and his sight will suffer from the poor light.

tempted him with stories that the work was easy, with free accommodation. Suriyan found himself sharing a small room with other children. There were no beds, and many children had to use the same toilets and washing facilities. All the children had to work ten hours a day. Inhaling the fumes of the glue and dyes used on the bags made them dizzy at first, but after a few months they became addicted.[24]

Fact File

Why children go to work in factories
A study of 180 working children, mostly girls between 10 and 16 years old in an industrial area near the Indonesian capital, Jakarta, found that they were employed in factories making cookies, mosquito coils, medicine, clothes, lightbulbs, and glass. They all came from large families in which, if two parents worked, the total income would not be enough to support the whole family. Most had dropped out of school. They gave these reasons for starting to work in factories:

Need to support the family	30.56%
Education is useless	19.44%
Wanted to join friends already working	18.89%
Parents forced them to go to work	12.22%
No money for school	7.78%
Couldn't understand school lessons	7.78%
School is too far away	3.33%

Source: *Child Workers in Asia*, Volume 7, No. 2, 1991

Child labor and big business

The work done by children makes money for the adults who exploit them. Children work in order to earn enough money for survival for themselves and their families. They may not be aware that they are also linked to large-scale industries making big profits—even in the case of ragpicking. Sometimes children form an important part of the workforce in factory-based industries, even when this is forbidden by law.

A young seamstress works in a Bangladesh textile factory. All the cloth produced here is sold abroad.

Carpetmaking is one major industry employing children, both in small workshops and large factories in India, Bangladesh, Pakistan, Nepal, and in parts of North Africa. This is so important to the exports of these countries that, as shown in chapter 3, it has been the subject of international campaigns to ban child labor. As in the case of the Thai leather bag industry, children often travel alone from rural areas to work in carpet factories. Sometimes they migrate on their own, but many are attracted by middlemen, some are kidnaped, and others are bonded laborers.

Life for child carpet weavers

One of the main Indian areas for carpet manufacture is Uttar Pradesh, where children work and live in the factories, sleeping at night on the floor of the same huts where they work the heavy looms during the day. Children can learn how to weave carpets in six months, but they are treated as learners

for far longer, maybe up to five years, during which time they are given food but no wages. Even when they are paid, 25 percent goes to the master weaver, who supervises their work, and up to 20 percent goes to the person who owns the loom. The children are employed because their labor is so cheap and they can be bullied into working for hours without a break. Child weavers are never as skilled or as fast as adults, but many people believe the myth that tying the knots on handwoven carpets can only be done by children's small fingers.

Child weavers may start at 5:00 A.M. and work at the looms until 7:00 P.M., with only one half-hour break. In the evening they still have to spend at least one more hour preparing for the next morning by sorting and winding balls of yarn. All day, they sit in an earth pit leaning forward to the looms, in

Girls in Nepal sometimes say that they prefer the work in carpet factories to the hard work that they had to do in their home villages. But working conditions are hardly ideal for the more than 150,000 children employed in making carpets for sale overseas.

Fact File

Children's views about carpet factories
In rural Nepal one way of coping with increasing poverty is for children to migrate to carpet factories in Kathmandu.

"Andheri is in the high hills…and is thought of as a very poor area, where children, especially girls, have very little opportunity to go to school and where the households are affected by deforestation [the clearing of trees] and landslides….The few boys from the area said they would prefer to be at home. However, the girls…said they would prefer to be in the factory, as factory work is easier than their work at home…

"This is in striking contrast with the perceptions of the children from Beltar. The local broker…pays the parents directly so the parents are assured of payment. All the children, however, said they would prefer to be in their village where they could play when they were not working, could get assistance with work from others, and could also visit relatives. In the carpet factory, they can never get help and they have to work continuously."

Source: V. Johnson, J. Hill and E. Ivan-Smith, *Listening to Smaller Voices: Children in an Environment of Change* (ActionAid, 1995)

poor light, breathing in fluff and dust. Their fingers become sore and their eyesight suffers. They are often subjected to physical punishment and verbal abuse.[25]

The effects of this kind of work are lifelong. A medical survey compared schoolchildren with carpet weavers of the same age. It found that schoolchildren were taller and heavier and suffered from fewer illnesses and injuries.[26] It is clear that child weavers will grow up to be smaller, less healthy adults. They also rarely go to school, so they are unlikely to be able to improve their lives. This happens because adults make profits from the work done by children.

Morocco's carpet industry is a major source of wealth for the country. Girls are apprenticed at a very early age, then lose their jobs in their teens when their eyesight fails as a result of the poor working conditions.

VISIBLE AND INVISIBLE EXPLOITATION

Some city children who work on the streets also live there, spending the night in doorways, in parks, under railroad bridges, curled up under market stalls, or in corners of bus stations. If the police find them they move them on, often violently. Children are not supposed to be out on the streets unaccompanied by adults. Modern city centers, where these children gather, are largely empty of people at night and the only adults found there tend to be other street people, prostitutes, or criminals. Children find it safer to gather in groups at night for protection, but their uncomfortable sleep is often broken by older youths and adults who molest them or steal their few belongings and, most often, by the police. If they are lucky, the children escape arrest. If not, they spend the rest of the night in a cell and are dragged away to prison among adult criminals or to be locked away in an overcrowded, unsanitary orphanage. Most street children have been in prisons or orphanages at least

A Moscow street boy in a house of detention, having been rounded up by the police. He will now be assessed to see what his future might be.

66 99
• • •

An eight-year-old Colombian street child said:

"The first night in the streets was very difficult. I felt very sad, but I was very angry at everyone. I imagined how other kids, who live in rich families, have everything. I felt I had nothing and that to be like them would be impossible. I was hateful toward them and everything. Then I slept and dreamed of returning to be born again as equal to the rest of the children."

Source: Lewis Aptekar, *Street Children of Cali* (Duke University Press, 1988)

Media Watch

Tamsin's story
"She was placed in the care of Devon Council at the age of ten. Her parents were separated and there was no one to look after her. When she turned 16 this summer she was on her own. She decided to take her chances in London. She clutches her two plastic bags, containing all the possessions she has accumulated in her lifetime…Her home now is the underground parking lot in Leicester Square and, occasionally, in Soho [London].

" 'It's cold out there, you're filthy dirty, and you're hassled the whole time,' says Tamsin. 'Basically it's totally degrading, you're treated like a piece of dirt.'"

Source: *Evening Standard,* December 1992

once, eventually escaping to the streets with relief. There they are free, even if they often cannot get food or a good night's sleep. However, it is not surprising that daytime can find them so exhausted that they fall asleep, barely noticing the city filling again with traffic and people.

(Left) Brazilian boys sleeping on the street. Children often prefer to live outdoors rather than return to poor or unhappy homes or to stay in orphanages or detention centers.

Life on the streets

Antonio and Pim are both 15 years old and have lived on the streets for over two years, but in very different parts of the world. Antonio lives in Mexico City, Mexico, while Pim left an unhappy home to go to Amsterdam, the capital of the Netherlands. They share many of the same problems. It is hard to get enough to eat, and people treat them badly, believing them to be criminals or drug users. It is easier for Antonio to find work because the streets of Mexico City are full of street traders. He has earned money selling newspapers and lottery tickets, as well as shining shoes. If he can't

Many street children sell newspapers to commuters. This Nicaraguan boy will have to share his profits with the adult who supplies the newspapers.

find shelter at night it is usually not a problem because the weather is mostly warm and dry. Pim, on the other hand, finds that from time to time he has to find help from the various coalitions for street children in Amsterdam, especially when the winter cold sets in. He goes from one shelter to another, trying to make the most of the services available, but he is unwilling to settle down or go home. Both boys steal sometimes. If he is caught, Antonio is likely to be beaten by the police and thrown into a harsh prison. Pim would be more likely to be handed over to social workers, who might make him go back home.[27]

Making a living

Some street children are directly exploited by adults who supply goods in bulk for sale and take the majority of the profits. In some cases, children even get drugs from adults to sell on the street, having been persuaded to try the drugs themselves. Once children are addicted to the drug, the adult does not have to give them any money, because they can be paid by giving them the drug they crave.

“ ”

• • •

Accept us
We are the children of the streets
Children whose hearts are pure
    by coming together, by being together
We get the inspiration to achieve.

Society has rejected us
that we too are humans, we shall but prove
bootpolishing, ragpicking are not dirty
    occupations
This is our service to society.

Do not look at us from afar
Come close to us

We are not what you think we are
Accept us.

Ravi Pednekar, *Poems by Street Children*
(YUVA, 1992)

(Right) Suresh is a street boy who lives under this bridge in Kathmandu, Nepal. He has to roast about 80 pounds of peanuts every day to earn just twenty rupees (55¢).

" ... "

Do studies help street children?

"Many of the [street] children in our study expressed concern regarding the actual benefits this study would bring them. Their wariness of the promises made to them by so many people in the past and their lack of faith in the government was revealed in statements such as:

"'How will this study help us?'
"'So many people have come and talked to us. But what have they done for us?'
"'What has the government done for us?'"

Reddy, N., *Street Children of Bangalore* (UNICEF, 1992)

Fact File

Drug use among street children

Throughout the world drug use is fairly common among street children. Cigarettes and alcohol use are the most common. Inhaling fumes from thinners, glue, and cleaning fluids is the cheapest form available. Marijuana is also used where it is cheap and easily available, as in India and some parts of South America. It is only in developed countries that young people living on the street use hard drugs such as cocaine (especially crack) and heroin. These drugs are expensive, and children have to steal or prostitute themselves to get the money to pay for them. A survey of street children in Nicaragua found that:

21% had some kind of addiction
70% knew that drug use could be damaging
71% of users would like to stop
29% of users wanted to continue using drugs.

Source: Connolly, M., *Survivors: The Health of Street Children and Youth* (UNICEF, 1995)

Windshield washers at traffic lights in Kingston, Jamaica, know that they have to work fast before the lights change and their customers drive away without tipping.

Some street children work for themselves. Ragpickers (see page 37) not only keep cities clean, but also provide materials for recycling, which are used to make large profits in various industries. If these industries had to pay proper wages to adults for collecting garbage, the profits would be smaller. Similarly, shoe shiners are not directly controlled by adults, but they are still exploited. They work to pay for their own upkeep and in some countries for their own education, which means that society does not have to pay. These are examples of the way in which the rich exploit the poor, especially regarding the exploitation of children.

Fact File

Working in the home

"Although in some countries boys perform a larger share of family labor such as herding livestock, with few exceptions girls do more home and marketplace work than boys. In Nepal and Java, most young girls spend at least a third more hours per day working at home and market than boys of the same age, and in some age groups as much as 85 percent more hours. In Malaysian households, girls age five to six who do home or market chores work as much as 75 percent more hours per week than boys of that age…

"Clearly, girls who work more than their brothers will be less likely to attend school, or they will be more overworked if they do (causing them to perform less well). In addition to lost work, parents in many countries feel that girls are foregoing important child care, household, and craft training at home if they go to school. In making education decisions, parents weigh the relative cost of opportunities against expected returns."

Source: King, Elizabeth M., *Educating Girls and Women: Investing in Development* (World Bank, 1990)

The exploitation of girls

Street children are particularly visible and attract public attention. They are often featured in newspapers, photographs, and on television. They are almost always boys. This does not mean that girls are not exploited when they cannot count on family protection, but this exploitation tends to happen where they are neither seen nor photographed—in other people's houses.

Very few children get through childhood without having to help around the house. Although this may be boring, it is also part of learning to be an adult and is, perhaps, as important as going to school. In many families across the world, parents believe this is especially important for girls. In poor families, if there is a choice about which children should go to school, it is likely they will send a boy, who may be able to use his education to get a good job and help the whole family. Many believe that girls will only get married and have children and that there is no point in sending them to school. Many girls never go to school, and some do not even learn to read and write.

Media Watch

Tamil girls

"Because of the simple fact that girls are not boys, girls have two jobs: one outdoors and one in the home. When the day's labor on the plantation is over, a boy can then enjoy not exactly leisure, but an absence of work—not so his sister.

"From as young as eight or nine, Tamil girls look after younger siblings during the day and so free the mother to work on the plantation. When the infants are older the juvenile nannies then graduate to their double labor. Some girls miss out on the nanny period altogether and go to work outdoors at eight years old."

Alan Whittaker in *Anti-Slavery Reporter*, 1987

African women do most of the farmwork. This Ivory Coast girl may never go to school because her parents probably think it is not worthwhile to educate a daughter.

Maids of all work

For many girls, a lack of education means that they are limited to housework and child care. In developing countries, girls frequently become "maids of all work," living away from their families and doing domestic work or looking after younger children, often when they are as young as eight years old themselves. Sometimes they travel to developed countries to take domestic jobs. Because they work in private homes, they do not get the public attention given to boys on the streets, but there are many million more girls working as servants— isolated, miserable, and hidden from public view.

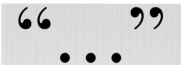

In search of the girl
"Girls are the most invisible among all the groups of invisible child workers. They are out of school, they are child minders and domestics. We have almost no information, and we need it."

Sheila Taçon, UNICEF, Botswana

Sometimes parents in rural areas where there is no school send daughters to work in the city, hoping they will be able to work as maids and pay for their education. This is what happened to 11-year-old Maria and her sister Patricia, aged 12, from Peru.[28] Maria and Patricia had to leave home when they began to grow too big for their parents to support.

They traveled to Lima on a battered bus with a distant relative who lived in the capital and promised she would find them work and schooling. "When I arrived in Lima I knew nothing," says Patricia. "The woman I work for taught me everything, the names of things, even how to buy bread. Everything was different, the customs, the food, the music. The house had so many rooms, so many things, electric gadgets I didn't know how to use."

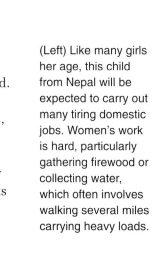

(Above right) Ruba cares for her baby sister in a slum in New Delhi, India. When parents are busy working, girls often miss out on an education because they have to stay at home to take care of younger brothers and sisters.

(Left) Like many girls her age, this child from Nepal will be expected to carry out many tiring domestic jobs. Women's work is hard, particularly gathering firewood or collecting water, which often involves walking several miles carrying heavy loads.

A typical day for 12-year-old Augustina, in Bolivia, starts at 6:00 A.M. when she goes out to buy food for the family's breakfast. Then she cleans the house, goes shopping again, and prepares lunch. "After that I have to wash the clothes, so I don't eat until 3:00 P.M. Then there is the ironing or something else. I go to school from 6:30 to 11:00 P.M., but I've never done my homework and when I get back, the señora scolds me. I still have to wash the dishes before I go to bed. I don't know what to do. How can I put up with this life? Is it like this for everyone, or just for me?" Augustina has no chance to make friends. She does not know that there are millions like her who have also lost touch with their families.[29]

Fact File

Conditions for domestic servants

"Payment to servant girls is often in kind. A 1990 survey of girls working as domestic servants in Lima [Peru], found that ten percent receive no salary at all, or only pocket money. The rest earn barely enough to cover basic necessities. Their food tends to be family leftovers, eaten after the employers have finished, off a plastic plate. Food and clothing sent by their families may be given to the children of their employers, but because they are not able to read and write, they cannot tell their families. Sleeping accommodation tends to be truly basic. One girl was found sleeping under the kitchen table, another in a windowless closet previously used for the family dog.

"Child domestic workers are normally on call 24 hours a day. Domestic workers of any age have little legal protection in Peru. There are no fixed hours. Time off for public holidays may be limited to Christmas Day, and even then may be cancelled at the whim of the employer."

Source: Ennew, Judith, *Juvenile Street Workers in Lima, Peru* (report), 1985

Girls and women work hard carrying bricks at a kiln in Nepal. After a hard day's work, it is usually girls and women who perform domestic duties like cooking and cleaning.

THE SEXUAL EXPLOITATION OF CHILDREN

Laws protecting children from adult exploitation are based on the fact that children are not yet fully grown physically, sexually, or emotionally. One of the strongest taboos in all societies is against adults having sex with children. Both boys and girls can suffer injuries from sex with adults or catch sexually transmitted diseases, including AIDS. Girls who become pregnant before they are mature may be severely damaged in childbirth. Above all, when adults use their power to force children into sexual acts, the children feel helpless. This emotional hurt may never heal. Nevertheless, some adults do pay money for sex with children. Others buy photographs that show children looking sexy or having sex with adults.

For sex between adults and children to be called exploitation, money must be involved, although sometimes children are given "gifts" or do not receive any cash at all because they are being sold by the owner of a brothel or a man who claims to protect them. Newspapers like to publish stories about the vast amounts of money that can be made through selling children for sex. Reality, however, is less dramatic. Child sex tends to be cheap and street children who work as prostitutes often suffer violent attacks

Fact File

Prostitutes from Nepal
According to the Indian Health Organization, there are about 100,000 girls from Nepal working in Indian brothels. Nepali authorities put the figure even higher. No one knows how many of these girls and women have been tricked or forced into crossing into India and entering this trade. But there is sufficient evidence that large numbers of young girls have been sold against their will and then raped and beaten in the brothels until they submit to the work. The number of girls who enter India illegally from Nepal every year is believed to be between 5,000 and 7,000, although not all become sex workers. Others end up in carpet factories.

Source: Omar Sattaur, *Child Labor in Nepal* (Anti-Slavery International, 1993)

These girls from a northern tribe in Thailand have been rescued from life in a brothel and are learning new skills.

Teenage girls from poor rural villages in northern Thailand travel to the capital, Bangkok, in search of work but often end up as prostitutes.

Fact File

Estimates of child prostitutes in some Asian countries
It is difficult to compare figures because the information is collected in different ways, the age of a child may differ from under 16 to under 21 years, and some countries only collect information about girl prostitutes.

Country	Number of prostitutes	Number of child prostitutes
Pakistan	200,000 from Bengal	20% of prostitutes are children
India	1.5–2 million	20% of prostitutes are children
Nepal	150,000 in Indian brothels	20% of prostitutes are children
Sri Lanka	30,000	mainly young boys
Vietnam		40,000 are children
Thailand		200,000–300,000 are children
Philippines		100,000 are children

Source: ECPAT, *The International Campaign to End Child Prostitution in Asian Tourism* (ECPAT, 1993)

from adult prostitutes who do not like their prices undercut. Even in brothels, the price of a child is not high. Youth and freshness are valued by the customers, but it is not expensive for brothel owners to lure children into this work and keep them working with threats and punishments. As in all cases of child labor, one of the main reasons for employing children is that they cannot defend themselves from exploitation.

Fact File

Sex tourism
Germany has passed a law that any German adults convicted of sexual exploitation of a child under 14 years old while in another country will be punished, with imprisonment or fines, when they return home.

There have been campaigns in other countries to try to pass similar laws, including Great Britain, Sweden, the United States, and Australia. In Sweden a 30-year-old law for crimes against children living overseas was used to convict a tourist who fled to Sweden from prosecution for sex crimes with children in Thailand.

Some tourists from developed countries are attracted to countries such as the Philippines, Sri Lanka, and Thailand by stories of the young boys and girls they can buy for sex. Boys can earn good money by hanging out on beaches or in tourist centers looking for customers.

A different story for girls

A girl prostitute is usually controlled by an adult. This may be a man who begins by pretending to be her boyfriend and then insists that she sleep with other men for money. Girls who have left home because they are unhappy often fall victim to such men, as do maids who have been thrown out because they are pregnant. They are exploited in three ways—by having to sell sex, by the way the men play on their emotions, and by being forced to give most of the money they earn to the "boyfriends."

Girls who are lured into brothels, often by female owners who are former prostitutes, are even less free. Sometimes they are not allowed out at all and are given none of the money they earn. Country

Fact File

Devadasi

In south India, the system by which girls are dedicated to temples is called *devadasi*. Daughters of low caste families are dedicated before puberty to the goddess Yellamma. On a single February day in 1990, 2,000 girls were dedicated in an open-air ritual. Those who did not remain in the temples to serve priests and male worshipers were sold in the sex bazaars of Bombay.

A study of 80 child prostitutes in Bombay found that:

5% earned 50 rupees [$1.50] a day
55% earned 100 to 300 rupees [$3.00 to $7.50] a month
33% earned more than 300 rupees [$7.50] a month.

They had been bought for between 5,000 and 8,000 rupees [$160 and $250]. Brothel owners pay nothing to the girls until this investment has been paid back.

Source: Patkar, P., "Girl Child in Red Light Areas," in *Indian Journal of Social Work* Volume 52, No. 1, January 1991

girls are easily persuaded to move to the city with promises of good jobs. Their parents may even be given a cash advance, which they take to pay off debts. Once in town, the girl is forced into prostitution. Her parents cannot return the money, and she cannot pay it back because the brothel owner gives her no wages. She is ashamed to go back to the village, and she is trapped.

(Above left) Underage prostitutes in Asia wait for clients to join them.

(Right) Rich tourists from developed countries are often the most sought-after customers for young prostitutes like this girl from Manila, the Philippines.

Media Watch

Law to follow child-sex tourism home

"Child prostitution is one of the saddest scourges in developing Asia. Every year thousands of men from Western Europe, the United States, and Australia fly into southeast Asia in search of children as sex partners or to use them in pornography. Some poor parents in developing countries sell their children into a kind of slavery, while governments desperate for tourist dollars turn a blind eye...

"Previously, efforts to control the trade have largely been a pitiful failure because of widespread corruption. Now, however, efforts around the world have been galvanized in a campaign to adopt stricter laws in the so-called consumer countries, to discourage men from venturing overseas for underage sex.

"The campaign is being spearheaded by a small group called End Child Prostitution in Asian Tourism [ECPAT]...

"'Tourism is providing the context in which the child abuse exists,' said Ron O'Grady, who was one of ECPAT's founders. 'You often find that the farther a traveler gets away from home the more they lose restraints.'"

Source: Charles Wallace in the *Guardian*, July 1994

Male prostitution

Both boys and girls work as prostitutes, but the patterns are different. Boys usually work alone and tend to form relationships with the men who give them gifts and money and may even take them into their homes for a while. Chito was 11 years old when he first met his American friend, Trevor, at the air force base where Chito's mother helped in the laundry. Until then, Chito had worked carrying heavy cans of water to the slums of Manila, the capital of the Philippines. Trevor gave Chito money, candy, and clothes. Then he invited Chito to his home and introduced him to the delights of luxuries like the shower and the television. Sometimes Chito fell asleep watching television. One day he woke up in bed with Trevor. Soon he learned what games made Trevor happy and that he had to keep them secret or his friend would get angry. The supplies of presents and money he took home were welcome. His parents did not ask why Trevor was so generous. Nevertheless, after a few months Trevor grew tired of Chito. He found other young friends and Chito was told not to come back. The little boy was miserable, and his parents were angry that there were no more gifts.[30]

Sri Lankan street boys are sexually exploited by tourists from Europe and North America.

Although poverty is related to prostitution, child prostitutes do not always come from the poorest families. People usually see themselves as richer or poorer according to what they think others have. Children in developed countries are encouraged by advertisements to think that they must have the latest and most fashionable clothing, gadgets, or entertainment. Such things are expensive, so some children from quite well-off homes sell sex in order to buy them, risking their mental and physical health. At the other end of the scale, children who live on the streets of developing countries have very few possibilities for gaining an income. Street life is not as active as it is elsewhere; there are few stalls selling food and goods where they can help and almost no shoeshining or car-washing opportunities, so they may be forced into prostitution just to get the money to eat. Although life is easier for street children in developed countries, many still turn to prostitution to make a living.

CHILDREN WORKING AGAINST EXPLOITATION

"If children had a voice, they would protest," said Thomas Hammarberg, a tireless fighter for children's rights, at a meeting on child exploitation in Geneva in 1993.[31] The fact is that children now do have a voice, at least in theory, through the articles of the UN Convention on the Rights of the Child, which give them the right to express their opinions and form groups to protect their own interests.

A history of organized protest

Organizations of working children are not new. Apprentices were an important part of the system of production and

Children in a math class in Lima, Peru, which is part of a local children's rights campaign.

trade throughout Europe before industrialization. In the eighteenth century, a boy presented a petition to the English Parliament asking for better education, and schoolchildren have gone on strike in the twentieth century. The problem then and now is that adults tend not to take children seriously.[32] One exception was the role played by schoolchildren in the struggle against apartheid in South Africa. South African children were prevented from having classes in their own languages, and their education was of an inferior standard to that provided for white children. By protesting these conditions, black children, some of whom even lost their lives, were among the leaders of the fight against this racist system.[33]

Taking responsibility

Perhaps because they have experience in taking responsibility in an adult world, working children have often been successful in joint efforts to improve their own lives.

Sometimes it is enough to form a group to work together, buying materials in bulk, finding a place to work, and sharing the profits. The group in Peru called MANTHOC encourages this but also helps children organize and run their own meetings to tackle community problems. In one slum, children decided that the main problems they faced were uncollected garbage and heavy drinking by their fathers. They ran a successful campaign against both, which made adults change their habits. MANTHOC has grown from small beginnings in 1976 to a national network in which working children regularly meet to share their problems and try to find solutions. Now there are contacts with similar groups all over South America, and international meetings of children take place every year.

Street children elect a political representative at a street children's center in São Luis, Brazil.

International action
Working children in West Africa also organize international meetings. Sometimes these are specialized, with meetings of maids or apprentices from different countries discussing their particular problems. Once a year on International Labor Day (May 1), there is a big gathering of child workers of all kinds in Dakar, the capital of Senegal. Children from many different countries take to the streets with banners, songs, and street theater to make their voices heard and to tell adults about their concerns. In India, children decided that April 30 should be a special Child Labor Day on which they hold public meetings and demonstrations. Children in India have also carried out their own investigations into accidents at work that resulted in child deaths. They have written reports and made official complaints to the government.[34]

Finding a voice

Governments do take notice of children once they have a voice. The national movement of street children in Brazil has been a force in that country's politics at local and national levels since 1986.[35] When the Honduran government decided in 1993 to change the law for children, they held public meetings for people from all walks of life. At one meeting, organized with the help of welfare workers, the children surprised all the adults present with the way they spoke and the ideas they expressed. Adult meetings were canceled to give children more time to air their views.

Children cannot be members of trade unions because they are under 18 years old, but they can form their own associations. They may be proud of the role they play in supporting their families and even want to claim the right to work. In a sense, they work because they refuse to starve or become helpless victims. They work to buy their own uniforms and schoolbooks so that they can be educated and change their own lives. Organizations of working children in South America, Africa, and Asia have shown that children can help themselves. Besides getting experience in running an organization and making decisions, these children also learn about the exploitative situations in which they are trapped and devise strategies to improve their lives. They are not afraid to voice their own opinions, defend their own interests, and demonstrate in public so that adults can learn the truth about child workers.

> " "
> • • •
>
> **Children's view of child work**
> Honduran children, including street and working children, commenting on their country's new children's law, said:
>
> "The work a child does must be appropriate to his age and capacities. It must never be an obstacle to study. We believe great efforts must be made to eliminate all forms of cruelty to and exploitation of the child. We believe it is parents, not children, who should work."
>
> From *Toward Freedom*, Volume 42, No. 7, November 1994

59

(Above) These children are demonstrating for "childhood not wages" on Carpet Children Day in New Delhi, India, in 1992. The event was organized by the South Asian Coalition on Child Servitude (SACCS), which freed the children from slavery in the carpet industry in northern India.

(Left) In 1989 lethal gas leaked from the Union Carbide plant in Bhopal, India, injuring and killing many people. Here, hundreds of children stage a demonstration in front of the Union Carbide offices, demanding medical treatment for children injured in the disaster.

❝ ❞ • • • Celebration of May 1—International Labor Day—by working children of west Africa, in Dakar, 1994

"On behalf of working children (maids, go-betweens, bus fare collectors, shoeshiners, ragpickers, bag carriers, car parkers, tourist guides, dockers…) in Dakar and other cities, we hereby proclaim to the President of the Republic of Senegal our grievances and proposals to improve the conditions in which we live and work.

"In view of:
- the insecurity of the work we do;
- the difficulties and hardships faced every day;
- the abuse of which we are often victims;
- the scant consideration and respect toward us as human beings.

"We ask for all of us:
- recognition of our work as part of our country's development so that we can take a full part in building a new Senegal;
- acknowledgment of the right to respect and dignity to which all human beings are entitled;
- to have equal access to basic education and professional training that is adapted to our daily work (such as evening classes);
- to participate in drawing up plans made on our behalf."

From *Jeuda* (the journal of ENDA-Jeunesse Action), 1994

GLOSSARY

AIDS Acquired Immune Deficiency Syndrome (AIDS). This disease, which can be caught through sexual activity, causes a breakdown of the immune system and ultimately death. Diseases caught through sexual activity are called venereal diseases.

apartheid The system of racial segregation and discrimination that was imposed by the government of South Africa in 1948.

bonded labor A system by which people are forced to work for a money lender or landlord to pay off a debt.

broker A person who arranges a contract between two people or groups of people.

brothel A house or other building where prostitution takes place.

castes Social groups, each of which has a different trade and a different position in society. It is not possible for people to change from the caste in which they were born, even by marriage.

developed country A country that is rich and industrialized. Sometimes called first world countries, these nations are generally better to live in than developing countries, but all nations have some poverty and areas of underdevelopment.

developing country A poor country that depends largely on agriculture and has few industries. They are sometimes called third world countries. However, even within poorer countries, there are groups of wealthy people who have lives more typical of those in developed countries.

environment The natural world, including physical features such as rivers and mountains as well as plants and animals.

ethnic group A distinct racial or cultural group.

exploitation Making unfair use of another person for material or financial advantage.

freedom fighters Rebels or terrorists fighting an organized army of a government.

human rights The standard of treatment all people should expect to receive from governments and other people.

informal sector Work that is not protected by employment law, the wages of which are not taxed by the government. Typically, informal sector jobs are insecure, underpaid and are carried out by the more vulnerable groups such as migrants, women, and children.

International Labor Organization Now one of the specialized agencies of the United Nations (UN), the International Labor Organization (ILO) is responsible for workers everywhere. It collects information about working conditions and tries to make sure that these are fair by encouraging governments to sign international agreements to set standards.

irrigate To water agricultural land using a system of collecting and distributing water through channels and pipes.

malnutrition A condition caused by a lack of the foods necessary to remain healthy.

migration The movement of people from one place to settle in another area or country. People may move for political, religious, or economic reasons, or because of war or environmental factors.

piecework Work paid for according to the amount produced. For example, an agricultural worker picking fruit would be paid for every pound of fruit collected.

plantations Large estates where, usually, only one crop is grown. This type of agriculture frequently uses large numbers of cheap workers who live on the plantation and are dependent on the owners.

prostitution The act of performing sexual acts for payment of money or goods.

ragpickers People who sift through garbage in the streets or in landfills, looking for items such as paper or metal that can be reused or sold.

recycling Reusing materials such as paper, plastic, and glass.

refugees People who are forced to leave their home or country and settle elsewhere due to war, famine, disease, or political or religious persecution.

shantytown An area of makeshift housing, usually made from any material that is readily available. Most cities in developing countries are surrounded by large shantytowns that often do not have resources like running water, sanitation, and electricity. Shantytowns develop when families migrate to towns or cities where there is insufficient affordable housing.

slum An overcrowded and unsanitary area of housing, usually on the outskirts of a city.

slumlord A powerful businessman who owns or controls a slum area.

sweatshop A factory where goods are produced using "sweated" labor—the labor of workers who are exploited. The workers usually work long hours for very low pay, often in dangerous or difficult conditions.

UNICEF United Nations Children's Fund (UNICEF) is a specialized agency of the United Nations, formed in 1945 to look after the children in Europe who had suffered in World War II. Since then, it has increasingly worked with children in developing countries, with money raised in developed countries.

United Nations The United Nations (UN) was formed in 1945, through an agreement between the countries that had fought in World War II (1939–1945). It was originally established to keep world peace, but has a number of special agencies with particular tasks, such as the ILO (unemployment), UNICEF (children), WHO (the World Health Organization), and UNESCO (education).

FURTHER INFORMATION

Nonfiction books

Chaiet, Donna. *Staying Safe at Work.* The Get Prepared Library. New York: The Rosen Publishing Group, 1995.

Colman, Penny. *Mother Jones and the March of the Mill Children.* Brookfield, CT: Millbrook Press, 1994.

Greene, Laura. *Child Labor: Then and Now.* Impact. New York: Franklin Watts, 1992.

Kronenwetter, Michael. *Under 18: Knowing Your Rights.* Issues in Focus. Springfield, NJ: Enslow Publishers, 1993.

Landau, Elaine. *Child Abuse: An American Epidemic.* Revised edition. Issues of the 90's. New York: Julian Messner, 1990.

O'Connor, Karen. *Homeless Children.* Overview. San Diego: Lucent, 1989.

Wormser, Richard. *Juveniles in Trouble.* Issues of the 90's. New York: Julian Messner, 1994.

For older readers

Black, M. (ed). *Street and Working Children: Summary report of an Innocenti Seminar.* New York: UNICEF, 1993.

Boyden, Jo, and Holden, Pat. *Children of the Cities.* Atlantic Highlands, NJ: Humanities, 1991.

Fyfe, Alec. *Child Labor.* Cambridge: Blackwell Publications, 1989.

The Convention: Child Rights and UNICEF Experience at the Country Level. New York: UNICEF, 1991.

Organizations

Defense for Children International—U.S.A.
21 S. 13th Street
Philadelphia, PA 19107

National Child Labor Committee
1501 Broadway, Suite 1111
New York, NY 10036

Save the Children Federation
54 Wilton Road
Westport, CT 06880

Sources of information

[1] Marcos's story was told in an essay he wrote in 1982. It is recorded in Ennew, J. and Milne, B. *The Next Generation: Lives of Third World Children*, Zed Books, London, 1989.

[2] A copy of the full text of the Convention on the Rights of the Child can be obtained free from UNICEF. Write to UNICEF, Information Division, 3 United Nations Plaza, New York, NY 10027.

[3] These and other indicators of child poverty can be found in *Children and Development in the 1990s: A UNICEF Source Book* (UNICEF, 1990). Other sources of information are the UNICEF annual reports—*The State of the World's Children* and *The Progress of Nations*.

[4] Sairoong's story is told in *Child Workers in Asia*, Volume 9, No. 4, 1993.

[5] Sona's story is told in *On the Street*, July 1993, and is quoted in "Street Children in Asia: An Overview," unpublished paper for the International Working Group for Child Labor, Bangalore, India (Concerned for Working Children, 1994).

[6] Burra, N. "Child Labor in India." *Social Action*, 36, 1986. *Social Action* is published by the Indian Social Institute, Lodi Road, New Delhi, 110 003, India.

[7] Defense for Children International *International Children's Rights Monitor*, Volume 9 (DCI, 1992).

[8] Sattaur, O. *Child Labor in Nepal* (Anti-Slavery International, 1993).

[9] Ennew, J. and Morrow, V. "Out of the Mouths of Babes" in Verhellen, E. and Spiesschaert, F. *Children's Rights: Monitoring Issues*. Published by Mys & Breesch, 1994.

[10] Pond, C. and Searle, A. *The Hidden Army: Children at Work in the 1990s*. Published by The Low Pay Unit, 1992.

[11] Pollack, S.H., Landrigan, P.J., and Mallino, D.L. "Child Labor in 1990: Prevalence and Health Hazards" in *American Review of Public Health*, No. 11, 1990.

[12] *International Children's Rights Monitor*, Volume 11, No. 4, Volume 12, No. 1, 1994/95.

[13] Anslemo, J. "After the War? I Would Like to Work in a Sweet Factory" in *International Children's Rights Monitor*, Volume 11, No. 4, Volume 12, No. 1.

[14] Ennew, J. "Child Soldiers: Serving or Working?" in *International Children's Rights Monitor*, Volume 2, No. 2, page 18 and correspondence in Volume 2, No. 3.

[15] *The Child Labor Deterrence Act* of 1993, Section 2(A), Subsection 9.

[16] *Child Workers in Asia*, Volume 9, No. 4, 1993; Poudyal, R. *International Efforts to Ban Products that Use Child Labor in South Asia: SARO Briefing Paper No. 1* (Save the Children, 1994).

[17] Wilk, V.A. "Health Hazards to Children in Agriculture" in *Child Workers in Asia*, Volume 9, No. 4, 1993.

[18] Tevis, C. 1992, cited in Wilk.

[19] Pollack, Landrigan, and Mallino.

[20] Cole, S. *Working Kids on Working* (Lothrop, Lee and Shepard Books, 1980).

[21] Inbarj, S. "Young Muscles Toil the Malaysian Rubber Estates" in *Child Workers in Asia*, Volume 9, No. 4, 1993.

[22] *Child Labor in Tanzania* (International Labor Organization, 1992).

[23] Brace, S. and Dodd R. "Recycling for Life, Not Life Style" in *Child Workers in Asia*, Volume 9, No. 4, 1993.

[24] *Child Workers in Asia*, Volume 1, No. 2, 1991.

[25] *Child Workers in Asia*, Volume 3, Nos. 2–3, 1987; *Patterns of Slavery: India's Carpet Boys* (Anti-Slavery Society, Child Labor Series, 1988); Juyal, B.N. *The Situation of Working Children in Uttar Pradesh* (Indian Social Institute, 1987).

[26] Mattoo, G.M., Rauf, A. and Zutshi, M.L. "Health Status of School Age Children Employed in Carpet Weaving in Ganderbal Block" in *British Journal of Industrial Medicine*, 43, 1986.

[27] The stories of Antonio and Pim were collected for this book by Brian Milne.

[28] The story of Maria and Patricia is taken from Ennew, J., *Juvenile Street Workers in Lima, Peru*, an unpublished report for Overseas Development Administration and Anti-Slavery Society, 1985. (They are also told in the *New Internationalist*, special issue on the girl child, edited by Maggie Black, 1993).

[29] Augustina's story is translated from *Asi ando, ando como empleada*, edited and published by MANTHOC, Pueblo Libre, Peru, 1992.

[30] Chito's story is told by Father Shay Cullen in *Child Workers in Asia*, Volume 6, No. 3, 1990.

[31] Quoted in *Toward Freedom*, Volume 42, No. 7, November 1994. For information on *Toward Freedom* publications, write to 209 College Street, Burlington, VT 05401.

[32] Morrow, V. "A Sociological Study of the Economic Role of Children," unpublished Ph.D., Department of Social and Political Sciences, Cambridge University, 1992.

[33] Jupp, M. *Children Under Apartheid* (Defense for Children International, 1987).

[34] The following organizations for working children encourage children to defend their own interests; they also publish information about the processes involved: The Concerned for Working Children (CWC), 303/2 L.B. Shastrinagar, Vimanapura Post, Annasandrapalaya, Bangalore 560017, India; MANTHOC, Corazeros 260, Pueblo Libre, Lima, Peru; ENDA Jeunesse-Action, BP 3370, Dakar, Senegal.

[35] Swift, A. *Brazil: The Fight for Childhood in the City* (UNICEF ICDC, 1991).

INDEX